Country Sampler's

Country Decorating Ideas The 1987 Collection

Country Sampler's Country Decorating Ideas
The 1987 Collection
© 1988 by Sampler Publications, Inc.
All rights reserved

Photography: Dick Kaplan
Design: Mark D. Mazur
Room Stylist: Sue Worthley

Published by Sampler Publications, Inc.
Country Sampler Books
Post Office Box 711
Glen Ellyn, IL 60138

ISBN 0-944493-03-3

Preface

Country is old and new, comfortable and easy, eclectic and right at home. It is part of our past and an expression of our individual values. Its popularity has been growing over the last ten years and continues to be the most popular decorating life style.

In this edition of Country Sampler's Country Decorating Ideas, The 1987 Collection, the editors of Country Sampler have gathered together the best decorating ideas from the last year. This collection is gathered for those who have just discovered Country Sampler and would like to take a look at what they've missed over the last year, and also for those who would like a hard-bound copy to keep on their coffee table.

In the following pages, we show you how to accessorize your home, building around that antique piece you found at a flea market or antique shop, or a hand-made reproduction purchased from a local crafter. You can see how to arrange items on a wall or around a drysink, hutch, or cupboard or how to make your living room, family room, kitchen, bath or bedroom cozier by adding a touch of country to your decorating scheme.

Keep this edition handy as a reference tool for decorating your home with country. Find the decorating scenes that appeal to you and watch for the pieces featured the next time you visit a country shop or craft fair. We hope you will have as much fun decorating in country as we did when we decorated the rooms you see here.

Table of Contents

Stairways

Navy and white wallpaper sets off the collections on this stairwell wall. Old and new pieces, pine brass scales, rakes, and other country gear make this an interesting look. The cat would like your opinion.

Living Rooms

An antique pine table centers this living room setting. Warm colors of beige and salmon with a touch of pale blue in the picture and table accessories make this a comfortable corner for a cute puppy.

Behind the sofa in the living room, an antique corner cupboard displays the owner's collectibles. Blue and white accents flow from furniture to wall to shelves. A eucalyptus wreath repeats the flower theme in the fabric.

From the chairs to the windows, blue and beige fill this country room. Rust accents are found on the shelf, table accessories, and pillow. A sewing box, filled with projects, waits on the chair for its crafty friend.

Old and new quilts, coverlets, and country friends surround an old pie safe in a living room corner. Plain walls and patterned accents give this room a simple country feel. A mini school desk has two bear students waiting for class to begin.

Dining Rooms

A corner cupboard displays collectibles in this dining room. Throughout the room, ducks and geese adorn the shelves, floor, and wall. An antique oak icebox stores extra dishes and tableware.

In this dining room, an antique bucket bench is used to display a collection of bears. The red and blue accessories complement the stenciling around the ceiling.

Family Rooms

The deep red color is repeated in the flag, mini antique chair, and harvest of apples in the bucket. A touch of Williamsburg blue completes the picture.

Folkart dolls on the pillows, couch, and in the wreath combine with mini houses and a checkerboard to fill each corner of this setting with a country feeling. A wagon parked as a coffee table holds accessories.

Nicholas & Son Ltd.

Williamsburg blue and white accessories stand out on the red brick background in this family room. Ducks and geese on the shelf, table, and wood carrier are accompanied by candles and quilts for a country look.

Pink, blue, and white, accented with flowers, make this a sunny setting all year 'round. Baby's breath, baskets, and bunnies enhance the mood. A floral print rug and chair complement the checked fabric tablecloth.

An antique wardrobe is a perfect place for storing the TV and stereo in this family room. The color of the old blue stain is also found in the accent pieces on the table and wall, and in the rug.

The rust and navy of the quilt wallhanging are repeated throughout this family room. Country dolls perch in the dry sink, on a stool, and on the couch. An antique trunk serves as a coffee table.

Kitchens

Navy, red, and white are repeated in this kitchen scene in the wall decorations and the tableware. Mini hearts on the wallpaper are also seen on the apron. Shaker grain baskets house a mini bear, and a peg rack holds baskets, buckets, and kitchen accessories.

Crisp blue and white, set off with pine, grapevine, and baskets, make this an inviting country kitchen. Old quilt pieces repeat the feeling found in the wall decoration. Whimsical dolls find a home in an old basket.

Mini apples in the wallpaper are repeated in the basket on the desk and on the grapevine wreath. Apples, blue homespun, checks, and hearts lend a country feeling to this kitchen.

A collection of grey enamelware adorns the wall as well as the antique pine washstand. Fruit in the basket enhances the wallpaper theme. Earth tones combined with a touch of blue make this a cozy kitchen setting.

Bedrooms

Bears, bunnies, and ducks fill the corners in this child's bedroom. A basket houses three prize "pets." Pink and blue bows, quilts, and wall decorations tie the room together. Two bunnies wait for their buddy to return to his coloring.

Tiny red flowers on a white background in the quilt are a close match to the wallpaper selected for this bedroom. Dried flowers on the shelf continue the theme. Cats are dressed in red and blue and repeat the color scheme.

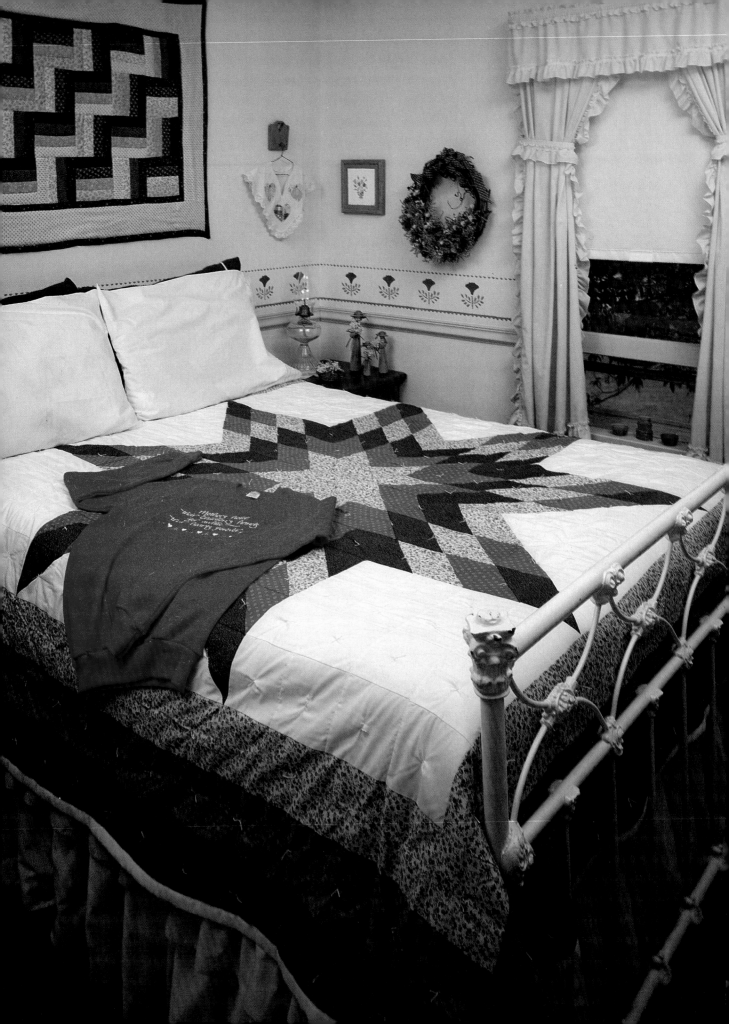

A bevy of bears on the shelves of an antique open hutch awaits its playmates. The colors of blue and white are repeated in the picture—the doll perched on the ledge, the quilts, and the Amish server. New and old trucks are used for housing toys and clothes, as well as for displaying favorite keepsakes.

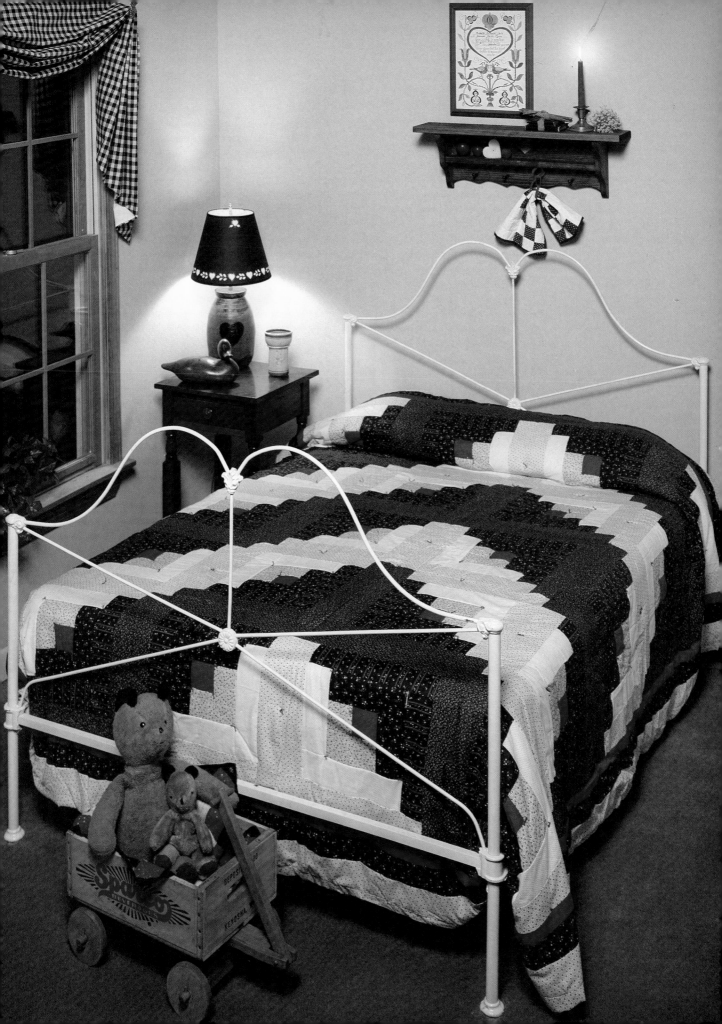

Pink and blue highlight a young girl's bedroom in the quilt shelf above the bed and bunny heart wreath. The blue candle and pink bow on the bear finish the picture.

In the bedroom, the four-poster bed frames a quilt filled with hearts. The predominant blues, with a touch of berry, also are found in the rope wreath and nightstand accessories. An old family bear nestles on the pillows.

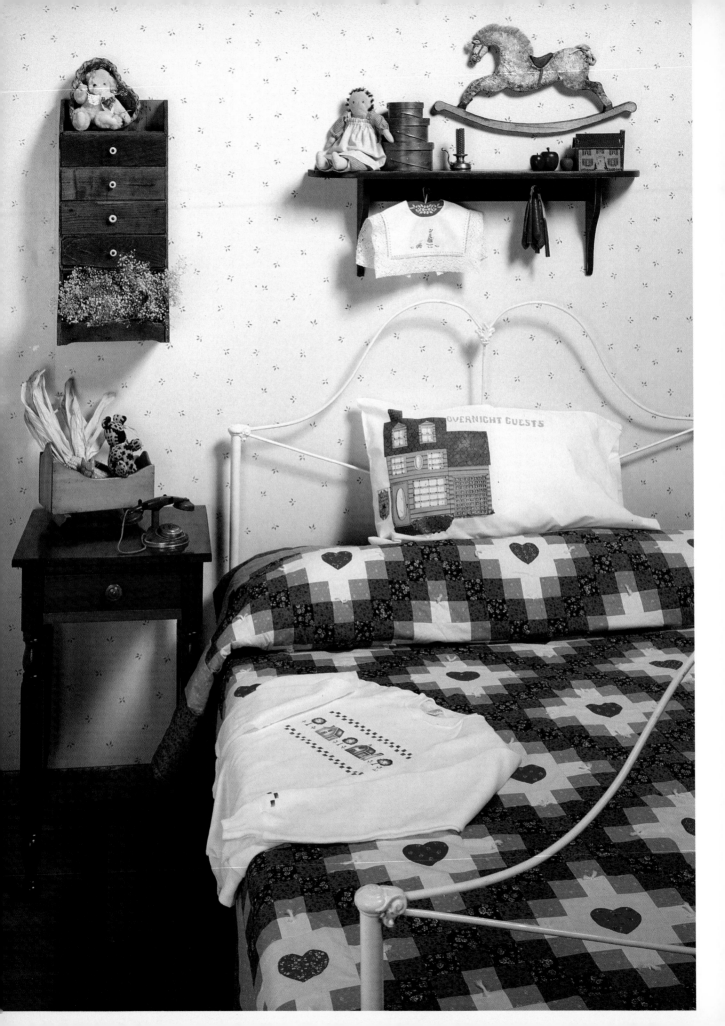

A primitive pine wardrobe is a perfect display case for old quilts. The contrast of navy and white is enhanced by pieces of antique pine furniture and sewing paraphernalia.

Christmas Givings

Antique doll quilts are centered on the wall rack. The Christmas bunny perched on a child's sled holds an old tin horn. The antique oil lamp gives a warm and inviting glow to this cozy setting.

MERRY CHRISTMAS

Better Homes and Gardens
LIVING
THE
COUNTRY LIFE

The simplicity of antique brass accessories and side boughs is enhanced by a collection of St. Nicks around the fireplace. A cozy fire welcomes guests at Christmastime.

Christmas red, blue, and a touch of green are found in the quilted stockings, bear in the wagon, and bunnies. The theme is repeated in the antique quilt, pictures, and arrangements of greens. Pheasant feathers and eucalyptus highlight the basket arrangement above the fireplace.

An antique pine washstand holds an old pantry box filled with popcorn. Gingerbread cookies, apples, and candy canes adorn the Christmas tree. Beneath the tree, gifts huddle in a basket, while a train awaits its engineer.

The colors of blue and cream are repeated in the coverlet, crock, and homespun curtains. The antique pine settle is accompanied by an antique flat-topped trunk that doubles as a coffee table.

COUNTRY
KID'S
Coloring Book